VITAL VITAMINS

Written by
John Wood

Published in 2022 by Enslow Publishing, LLC
29 East 21st Street, New York, NY 10010

Cataloging-in-Publication Data

Names: Wood, John, 1990-.
Title: Vital vitamins / John Wood.
Description: New York : Enslow Publishing, 2022. | Series: Brain food | Includes glossary and index.
Identifiers: ISBN 9781978523845 (pbk.) | ISBN 9781978523869 (library bound) | ISBN 9781978523852 (6 pack) | ISBN 9781978523876 (ebook)
Subjects: LCSH: Vitamins in human nutrition--Juvenile literature. | Nutrition--Juvenile literature.
Classification: LCC QP771.W66 2022 | DDC 613.2'86--dc23

Designer: Jasmine Pointer
Editor: William Anthony

Printed in the United States of America

CPSIA compliance information: Batch #CSENS22: For further information contact Enslow Publishing, New York, New York at 1-800-398-2504

Find us on

PHOTO CREDITS

All images are courtesy of Shutterstock.com, unless otherwise specified. With thanks to Getty Images, Thinkstock Photo and iStockphoto.
Scientist character throughout – Designbypex.
Cover – Kovaleva_Ka, indigolotos, AmyLv, New Africa.
4–5 – margouillat photo. 6–7 –marekuliasz, Toey Toey.
8–9 – Littlekidmoment, Jacek Chabraszewski, Brent Hofacker, 5 second Studio. 10–11 – ajlatan. 12–13 – Julia Mikhaylova, Jorge Salcedo. 14–15 – Valentyn Volkov, wavebreakmedia. 16–17 – MaraZe, Asada Nami.
18–19 – Poring Studio, Asada Nami. 20–21 – Evgeny Karandaev, Adriana Iacob, Moving Moment.
22–23 – AS Food studio, Brent Hofacker, Baevsu, Veronika Idiyat, ifong.

CONTENTS

Words that look like <u>this</u> can be found in the glossary on page 24.

A SLICE OF SCIENCE

Do grown-ups keep trying to feed you green vegetables? Do they question you for eating sweets? You might be wondering: why does it matter what I eat?

Hello!
I'm a small scientist.
I'm here to teach you about food. Food is very important!

You might have heard the words "healthy diet." A diet is the kinds of food you usually eat. To have a healthy diet, you need to make sure you eat different kinds of food.

A healthy diet is often called a **balanced** diet because you eat lots of different types of food.

PORTIONS

How do we <u>measure</u> the amount of food? A portion, or serving, is the amount you eat in one sitting.

Sometimes portions are measured in ounces. Use a food scale like this to find out the portion size.

A portion of food might be 16 grapes or a stalk of celery.

Different foods have different portion sizes. You should have five servings of fruits and vegetables a day. A serving of fruit is roughly the amount you can fit in the palm of your hand.

WHAT ARE VITAMINS?

Vitamins are found in food. Your body needs vitamins to work properly. There are lots of different types of vitamins that we need, so it is important to eat lots of different healthy food.

Let's have a look at some foods that give you lots of vitamins.

Milk

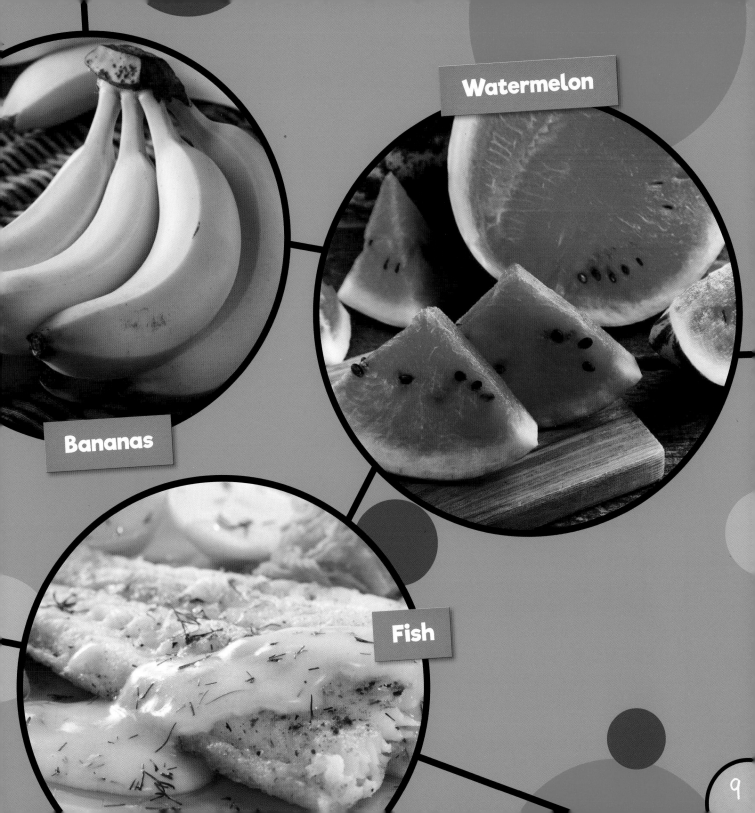

Bananas

Watermelon

Fish

9

LET'S EXPERIMENT!

This mood bar will tell us what's happening in the body. It shows four things — how quickly the body heals, how healthy the eyes are, how tired a person is, and how strong their immune system is.

HEALING

EYES

ENERGY

IMMUNE SYSTEM

HEALING

EYES

ENERGY

IMMUNE SYSTEM

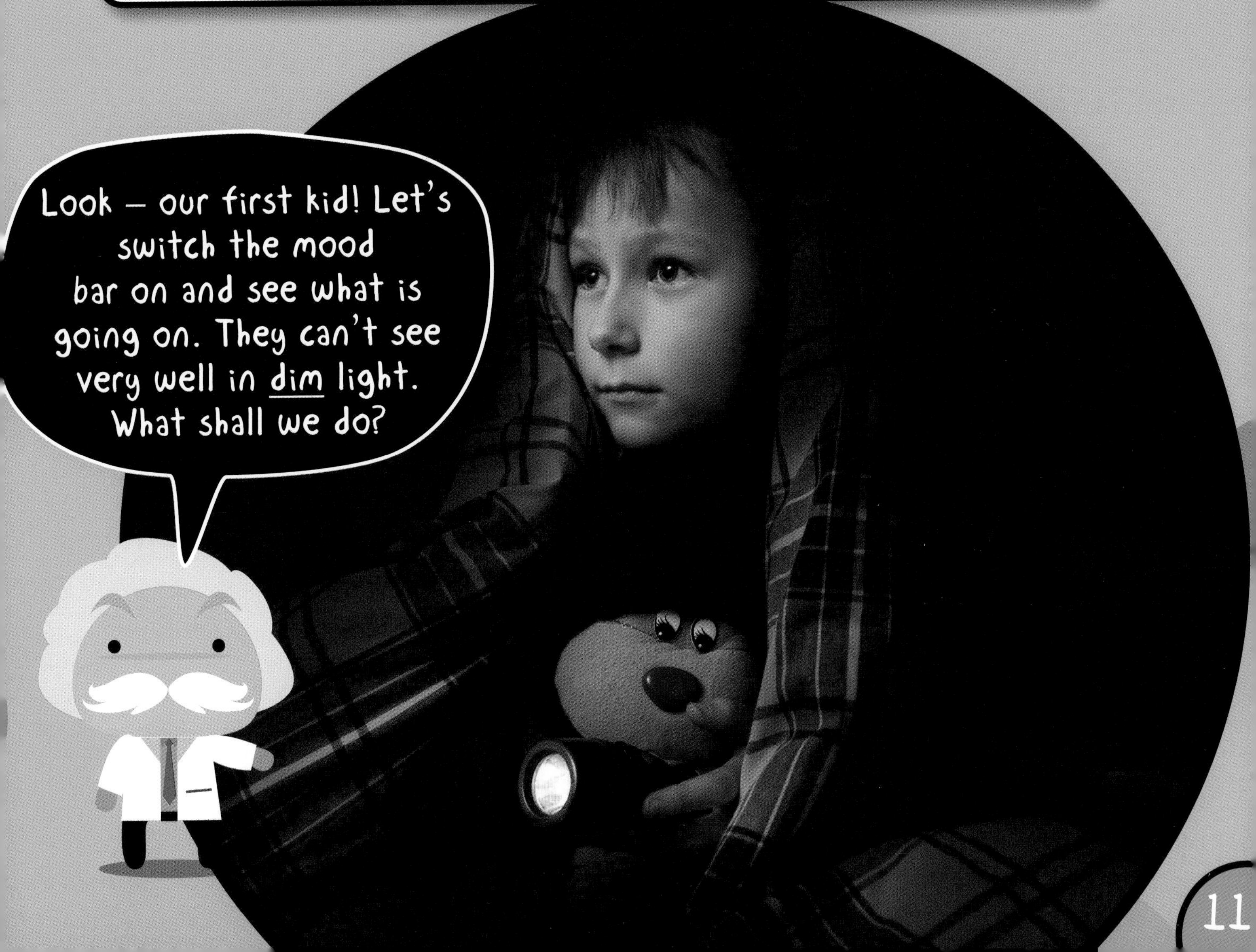

VITAMIN A
OK

We need spinach right away! Spinach is full of vitamin A, which helps you see in dim light. It is also good for your skin and makes your immune system strong.

HEALING

EYES

ENERGY

IMMUNE SYSTEM

Let's see how our next kid is doing. The mood bar shows that it takes a long time to heal when she gets a cut. How can we help?

VITAMIN C

YOU LATER, CUTS

Feed this girl an orange! Oranges give you vitamin C. Vitamin C is very important because it helps your body heal faster.

Citrus fruits, such as oranges, have lots of vitamin C.

BE HEALTHY, B12

Some people don't eat foods that come from animals. Healthy foods that don't come from animals are on page 20.

The boy could eat meat, such as beef or chicken. Foods that come from animals have vitamin B12 in them. Without enough B12, some people can feel very tired and weak.

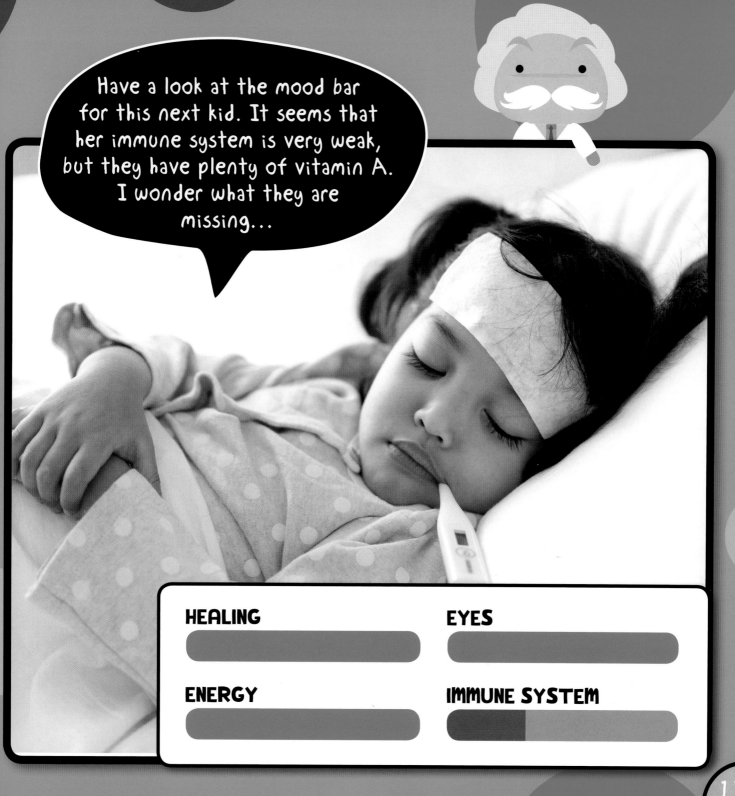

VITAMIN E IS A JOLLY GOOD
FELLOW

I know – they could have some nuts! Nuts, such as almonds and hazelnuts, give you a lot of vitamin E, which <u>strengthens</u> your immune system. This will help your body fight off illnesses and <u>infections</u>.

Almonds

HEALING

EYES

ENERGY

IMMUNE SYSTEM

As you can see from the mood bar, this kid looks healthier now. This was the best experiment ever. Well done!

FOOD SWAPS

Meat comes from animals. For example, beef is meat from a cow.

Some people are vegetarians, which means they don't eat animals. Vegans are people who do not eat anything that comes from animals, including eggs and milk.

Vegans and vegetarians need to make food swaps to get vitamins that most people get from animals. <u>Fortified</u> cereals are a good way to get important vitamins, such as vitamin B12.

Fortified cereal

wheat biscuits

FORTIFIED with VITAMINS & IRON+

made with WHOLE GRAIN WHEAT

Here are more foods that give you lots of vitamins to keep you healthy.

Potatoes

Mushrooms

Chickpeas

Broccoli

THE MOST IMPORTANT THING

Vitamins are very good for you, but don't forget that you must eat lots of different types of food. This is what makes a diet healthy and balanced!

Carbs

Fruits and vegetables

Protein

Fats and sugars

Dairy

GLOSSARY

balanced	made up of the right or equal amounts
citrus	certain types of fruit, such as oranges, lemons, limes, and grapefruit
dim	without a lot of light
fortified	made stronger, better, or more protected by adding something
immune system	the system that your body uses to defend itself against illness
infections	illnesses caused by dirt, germs, and bacteria getting into the body
measure	to find out the exact amount of something using units or systems, such as ounces for weight or feet for distance
strengthens	makes stronger

INDEX